Backup Fanatic

How to Ensure Business Continuity by Delivering Continuous Protection, Secured Storage, Data Compliance, and Instant Data Recovery

Domenic DiSario

Backup Fanatic
141031-001

Published by:
90-Minute Books
Newinformation Inc
302 Martinique Drive
Winter Haven, FL 33884
www.90minutebooks.com

Copyright © 2015, Domenic DiSario

Published in the United States of America

ISBN-13: 978-1502816955
ISBN-10: 1502816954

No parts of this publication may be reproduced without correct attribution to the author and the domain www.backupfanatic.com.

Dedication

To my wife Debra

And

"The Team"

Other books By

Domenic DiSario

Technology as a 2nd Language

Meditations for Geeks (late 2015)

Here's What's Inside…

Prologue 7

Introduction 11

Backup Fanatic! 13

The Distinction between Business Continuity and Just Having a Backup in Place 15

Why Don't More Businesses Have Business Continuity Plans in Place? 21

The Different Types of Disasters That Can Strike Any Business 27

Beware the "Head in the Sand" Business Continuity Strategy 31

Why Disaster Can Strike at Any Businesses 35

How to Protect Your Business from a Disaster 41

The Importance of Reliable Data Recovery (White Paper) 43

How to Protect Your Personal Data in the Event of a Disaster 59

How Old Technology Can Expose You to Risk 73

Proof Disaster Can Strike Twice 79

Here Are the Mistakes to Avoid When Doing Your Disaster Recovery 83

Frequently Asked Questions (FAQs) 87

Should Ask Questions (SAQs) 91

Myths 95

How to Find Out If You Are at Risk from a Potential Data Loss 99

Here Is How to Ensure Your Business Is Protected from Disaster 101

Protecting Your Personal Data... True, Hard Facts About Data Loss 103

Epilogue 109

About the Author 113

Postscript 115

Prologue

February 15, 2015

It's 10 AM Sunday morning.

Sitting in our comfortable family room drinking a cup of coffee as my wife plays "ballie" with the dogs in the background, there are a couple of things of note:

1) I feel very fortunate that we still have power (so far) after another foot of snow last night and this morning. We've totaled about 7 feet of snow in the last 3 weeks.

2) The dogs, who are both Border Collies, have a major case of "cabin fever" (me too).

Over the last few weeks there have been some extraordinary events as a result of this historic weather.

- The MBTA is closed again. This is unprecedented and causing lots of grief as people are unable to get to work.

- Although the Governor keeps encouraging people to work from home, some people just don't have that capability. Even though it seems unbelievable, not everyone has high speed Internet access, and, even more incredibly, some companies do not allow people to work from home. And even if they do, these corporate systems are only configured to allow a percentage (sometimes small) of their workforce to access corporate IT resources. We have received numerous calls over the last few weeks from companies looking for a better way and a more robust remote access strategy.

Of course, some folks can't work from home due to the nature of their work but they still need to check their work email on their mobile devices before they get in the car for the longest commute imaginable or as they sit freezing on the public transportation platform.

- Snowiest month on record in Boston! Between February 1, 2015 and February 15, 2015 almost 60" of snow fell. The previous record? 43.3 inches (Jan 2005). And we're only 2+ weeks in!

From *Boston Business Journal*

This book was written months before the snow of this winter and I have said many times that it does not take an earthquake, fire, hurricane or even a flood to grind many businesses to a halt.

A simple lack of access to the workplace is many times enough to bring a business to its knees. We are all susceptible one way or another.

From *The Boston Globe*

Introduction

Backup Fanatic

Boston, MA
March 2015

Being in the business world for so long, I have seen too many tragic stories of organizations mishandling their all-important data. I have seen everything from major businesses losing their entire client database to my next-door neighbor who lost her precious photos of her grandchildren.

We live in a data-driven society linked to our electronics. The ramification of losing all or even a portion of your data is enormous. I wanted to create awareness of how we ignore the inevitable data loss problem and how we must protect our data, both personally and professionally, from events that will cost your organization time and money.

It is no longer just about protecting data from a bad hard drive or a serious power surge, because now there is absolutely no flexibility in the time a business can take to get back to normal operations. Only a handful of businesses can tolerate even ½ a day without email!

The threats go beyond physical damage to data as well. Harmful computer viruses are more sophisticated than ever and can wipe an entire database in a matter of hours. Employee errors or bad acts can literally shut down your operations, destroy your reputation and cause you to lose your job.

How prepared is your organization right now? As the world becomes more and more dependent on having the right data available, you have to be diligent in your approach to protecting one of your organization's most precious resources – the all-important data and access to it on which your company's existence depends.

What follows is a transcript, along with supplemental material, in which I share with you the threats and challenges to your data integrity and availability of your IT resources and what you can and should be doing about those threats.

I hope this book is both educational and transformative. I want to teach you a bit about data security and change the way you think about your business continuity in the face of a disaster or lack of access. By the last page, you'll find yourself becoming a backup fanatic as well.

Take Good Care,

Domenic DiSario

Backup Fanatic!

Susan: Good afternoon, this is Susan Austin, and I am excited to be here with backup fanatic Domenic DiSario. Domenic is going to be sharing with us his thoughts and ideas on how businesses can avoid disaster by having a solid plan in place should the unthinkable happen. Welcome, Domenic.

Domenic: Thanks, Susan. Good to talk with you again.

Susan: Why do you call yourself a backup fanatic?

Domenic: Well, I have been in the IT Support business for a long time and have seen so many sad stories come down the pipe. Data backup is a very, very important part of any company's IT planning and, these days, any personal planning, because we really are a data-driven, data-dependent society.

What is curious is that we are dependent on our electronics, yet we approach backup naively, expecting devices to be 100% reliable, 100% of the time.

I mean, if you think about it, the half-inch thumb drive in my pocket holds 500 times more data than was on the first hard drive of the first PC I built. The ramifications of that are enormous, and we need to consider the end results of losing it. There could be regulated data on the drive. There could be my QuickBooks file with business records, my photos, my wife's genealogy research or scanned house records and they all matter and are impossible to replace from original paper sources since no one prints a paper copy of an electronic file anymore. (nor should they...).

In essence, backup, business continuity, and disaster recovery are critical in our lives and for some of us who work in a regulated environment are legally mandated. Added to this mix are mobile devices where the personal and the professional demarcation is gone forever.

The Distinction between Business Continuity and Just Having a Backup in Place

Susan: What are the distinctions between business continuity and a backup?

Domenic: With a backup, I am simply making a copy of a file or directory and in some cases, an application, whatever the case may be, and storing it somewhere else.

Data is typically backed up. The applications typically are not because they are tightly integrated into the various operating systems. So if I backed up my Microsoft Excel, I could not restore it. It would not work, so it would be useless to back up most applications. These days the application provider requires a download of the application since they don't provide backup CD's anymore.

The strategies in the past were always 'back up your data and we'll reinstall the applications' and that's still the case for most companies who do file and directory backup, and regrettably that's the extent of most companies' business continuity strategy.

Business continuity, on the other hand, is a disaster recovery solution and consists of a couple of parts. The first component is a local backup. Some companies have Internet-only backup meaning their data is residing in the cloud and when you need to recover it, it's going to take a very long time. A prudent course is to have a local backup as well in case your internet access is disrupted or your cloud provider experiences a service interruption. The thinking behind these two components is this:

Your server goes down for some reason. Your server is going to go down or crash more times than your building is going to burn down or get blown away by a hurricane, right? So a local backup is important because if your server crashes, you have a local copy of your data and I can recover it for you very quickly.

The second part of the solution is the offsite backup or cloud backup, so if your building does burn down, and your backup burns down with it, your files will still be saved although the restore time will be longer.

With file and directory backups, whether local or offsite, the road to recovery is cumbersome and long, so these types of backups are not terribly effective if you want to do a rapid recovery. They are perfectly fine if you want to wait a day and a half for your data, but most companies do not.

Fortunately, an image-based backup can remedy this problem. An image-based backup takes a complete image of your server, a point-in-time image, like taking a picture. That server, the data and applications can be recovered in their entirety at that point in time by simply restoring the whole image. The whole server is restored intact, including applications, patches, and data up to that point in time.

We need a local backup. We need an offsite

backup, and we need recovery capability. This is what makes a business continuity solution rather than just a backup protocol.

Server recovery capability means that an image is on a backup device and the image is made usable so that users can connect to it and start working. The reason that this is possible is the backup device is also a server.

For a typical client, we recommend backing up every hour locally and a couple of times a day offsite. Some of our clients, where it's mandated, back up more often. We back up as often as every 15 minutes, so worst-case scenario on most days is losing 15 minutes of data.

But now we don't just have a backup of the data, we have an image of that server. What time is it now—2:30? I can have an image of your server as it looked at 1:30. I can mount that image in its entirety and people are working off a 1:30 version of their complete server.

These components are the basic elements of IT business continuity. Business continuity means that in the event of some type of disaster, from an IT point of view, business is able to continue. Someone tells me, "My server crashed," and the first thing we say is, "Let's reboot." If it comes back up, great, and if it doesn't we can rapidly assess our options.

How long is it going to take to bring your business back up? Can I get this server working in 10 minutes or is the hard drive gone? If it is we will be able to spin up the last backup which is the image-based backup. Now the users will work off that, and I can fix that server without compromising your operations.

Now, if I need a hard drive or power supply or whatever the case might be, I have time. I can do the remediation off-hours or I can do it on the weekend because my users are working. When we finally repair that server, all the changes that were made to that virtual server, all the changes to the data, are actually copied back to the physical server. It's called the bare metal recovery. It allows me to take that virtual representation of your server and copy it back to the physical server as it stands at that minute. There is never any data lost.

That is business continuity to fix a local issue—a server crash or malware outbreak. This solution applies when your backup device or your backup appliance is still intact. But let's say you have the fire, flood, or hurricane situation. Now your whole building is gone. What are you going to do?

This is where the offsite copy of your data comes into play. If we had to copy all the data from the cloud it could take many, many hours, days, weeks, to get that data back, but in this scenario, we don't have to copy the files from the cloud server down to the local destination. We have the same image that is on the local device. We have a replicated image in the cloud. We simply mount that image in the cloud and people can connect to that server.

In the case of a fire, flood, or hurricane in which you lose the whole building, you might lose a dozen servers, but we can spin all those servers up in the cloud, and people can connect to their IT infrastructure from wherever they are. They could be home. They can be in Starbucks. They can be in a vacation house in Hawaii. They will be able to connect to this cloud representation of their data infrastructure.

Think about this. If your building burned down, and you had a business continuity solution in place, the worst possible ramification (from a data perspective) would be the loss of a half a day's data, and you'd be up and running in less than an hour. From a data-loss standpoint, that is not a bad end result of your building burning down.

Business continuity solutions aren't only helpful in the event a server is destroyed. I don't know where you live Susan, but the weather over the last few years has seemed to contain a lot of 100 year storms.

So when people can't get to work or the power is down in a building for any substantial amount of time, we spin up these servers in the cloud and people can work from wherever they are in a replicated version. Naturally, we need to get the changed data back down, but again, this can all happen during off-hours. Business continuity means that I need to keep everyone working, and we are able to accomplish that.

Why Don't More Businesses Have Business Continuity Plans in Place?

Susan: Why do you think many businesses aren't already protected? You would think, in this modern day and age, this would not be an issue.

Domenic: Yes, you would think that, but, unfortunately, this is not the case. One of the big reasons for this is simple unawareness. Often the folks who approve the expenditure don't really understand the risks or they may tolerate more risk than is really wise. They don't understand the recovery process and what it would take to get the systems and data back if they were fortunate enough to have even backed up their data in the first place.

I think businesses don't properly protect their data because they overestimate the cost of the fix and underestimate the cost of the failure. The cost of storage has plummeted and there are plenty of relatively inexpensive and scalable backup solutions so that anyone can afford to protect their data to ensure their business continues to go on in the event of a disaster.

From our Blog...

A Good Backup Strategy Could Save Your Business

Ahhh backup... It's messy, unreliable, prone to failure and the log file reporting is cryptic (to say the least). The hidden costs for managing a tape or hard-disk-based backup solution are unbelievably high. But backup is critical. It is not an overstatement to say that **<u>a successfully recovered backup could save your business.</u>**

10 Things to think about when evaluating your backup strategy.

1)   It's not about the backup. It's about the RECOVERY.

If you don't do regular test restores of various files (monthly) and full server recoveries bi-annually, there is no real way to know that your backup/recovery strategy will work when you most need it.

2)   It needs to be affordable.

One way to control costs is to revisit your procedures annually. Emerging technologies are providing more affordable and effective options. Solutions that were cost prohibitive only a year ago are now very affordable.

3)   If you are still using tapes as your primary media, STOP.

Tape drives are mechanical devices prone to failure. The tapes themselves have a relatively short shelf life (6-12 months) and are affected by environmental conditions like heat, humidity and magnetic interference.

4)   Don't forget offsite components in your planning.

Backup/recovery plans should include local backup for convenient restoring of files and other data in the day to day business environment. Offsite and secure copies of your data should also be readily accessible in the event of a disaster situation or in the event a critical server failure (see virtualization below).

5) Are you backing up everything you need and is it recoverable?

Too often we are called to restore data, only to find it is not recoverable because employees were not trained to follow backup procedures. This is especially prevalent with SQL (and other) database products as well as Exchange and other email systems.

6) Does your backup/recovery plan include a strategy in the event of a down server?

Can business wait for recovery? For some of us, each hour of down time comes at a high cost. In some backup plans, even in the best of circumstances, the company can expect a day down with the solutions they have in place. In that scenario, it may be time to think about solutions such as server virtualization, bare metal recovery capability, or an in-house spare server.

7) Retention needs to be considered.

Retention, archiving, and data availability must always be kept in mind (depending on your industry and the regulations that govern your long-term storage requirements). Also, some data you simply want to keep longer for reference. Review your overwrite and destruction plans at least annually.

8) Is once a day enough?

Take a good look at your backup schedule. Is it enough to back up just once a day? If you back up overnight and lose a key file at 2 PM, can you live with a copy from the day before? The capability to do incremental snapshots of your key data during the day is an important part of any backup/recovery strategy.

9) Backed up data needs to be secure (encrypted).

Whether you are using tapes, USB drives, or NAS sub-systems, your data needs to be encrypted. Not only to comply with various governing bodies, but also because it's just plain good business to have your data protected in the event it is stolen or lost. If your backup data contains information that is considered protected (e.g., name and social security number or patient health information), it is imperative to review accessibility from non-authorized users. In addition to HIPAA and Sarbanes Oxley, many states have specific data protection regulations that require logging of data access and backup logs in case of a data loss..

10) "Who is responsible?" (And a few other questions to ask yourself.)

Responsibility for the entire backup process should be clearly defined. Who is responsible for the actual backup process? Who monitors your backup? If your backup fails, when do you know it and what do you do? Who decides how the recovery will take place? When was the last time you tested your backed-up files? Where is the report? Where is the backup media? It's critical to have the answers to all these questions in writing!

Solid disaster recovery and business continuity planning is an integral component of any well-managed business, so spend the time to investigate new backup solutions and strategies. You will spend less IT money on a new approach and get many times the security and functionality.

For more information, visit:
http://backupfanatic.com

The Different Types of Disasters That Can Strike Any Business

Susan: Can you share with us some of the types of disasters you're talking about here?

Domenic: Sure. Fires, floods, anything weather related, which includes tornados, hurricanes, and tsunamis. You say tsunami here in Massachusetts and people just roll their eyes, but on the West Coast it's a serious concern.

Other less obvious disasters include power failures, and malware outbreaks. Just recently, there was a Cryptoware outbreak where hackers broke into business systems, encrypted their data files, locked them, and then charged them money to decrypt their files.

For a few of our clients hit by Cryptoware, we were able to restore a backup that immediately preceded the outbreak. The more completely and frequently you back up your data, the more current your restore point could be. Having a business continuity plan in place is paramount these days.

From our Blog...

Watch Out for the New CryptoWall 2.0 Ransomware Threat

Few things are as terrifying in this technologically advanced world as the thought of someone gaining access to your computer files and holding them hostage. Ransomware, or malware designed to do just this, is unfortunately more prevalent than ever. CryptoWall has been viciously lingering on the sidelines as a silent threat for some time now, and the situation is even worse with the release of CryptoWall 2.0, which makes it far harder to sidestep extortion and recover your own files.

Scammers with this new-and-improved ransomware attach CryptoWall 2.0 in ZIPs masquerading as PDF files in mass email campaigns. When opened, this program attacks your computer by encrypting all documents and pictures found on the hard drive. With CryptoWall's previous version, it was possible to recover your encrypted files without paying the requested $500 ransom or apply someone else's payment to your own. This is far more difficult, and sometimes impossible, with the new version of this menacing malware.

Here's how it works: when the ransom request is sent, a link is provided to pay the costly fee via bitcoin and get the computer files back. Each computer hacked is sent an individual link with a unique address, preventing the application of another's payment to one's own. CryptoWall will even delete your original files, making it more difficult to use data recovery software. Finally, this new version of ransomware uses its own dedicated TOR gateways, so scammers can effectively hide from authorities and prevent being blacklisted.

So, what should you do to prevent such an attack on your computer? First, do not open attachments from unknown senders. If, however, you inadvertently open and unleash CryptoWall into your PC, you may be among the lucky few if you act quickly. In some cases, downloading and installing CryptoWall removal software will do the trick. Otherwise, you'll have to rely on any backup files you may have or restore your files using a shadow copy restore (if you have that feature enabled).

Having a solid backup solution in place in some cases is the only way to recover your data. Make sure that you do and make sure you test the recovery process often!

For more information, visit: http://backupfanatic.com

Beware the "Head in the Sand" Business Continuity Strategy

Susan: Do you find, Domenic, that in a lot of organizations, unless they have had firsthand experience with some major data catastrophe, don't allocate the necessary resources to be properly prepared to restore their data?

Domenic: Yes, as I've noted people often underestimate the risks. But I think this is just human nature driving the lack of prudent business planning. Many organizations follow the head-in-the-sand strategy. On an intellectual level, people understand they could be in big trouble if they lose their data, but denial creeps in. It's the human condition, and I have sat down with people in multi-hundred-million dollar businesses, and they tell me, "The risk is pretty low and we'll take the risk" as if gambling the company's ability to operate on the most basic level is the sign of an assertive confident leader.   And I just look at them, and I say, "It is going to happen. It may not happen to you, it may not happen today, but it is going to happen to someone today."

Someone's building will burn down today. Someone's building will flood today. There will be a storm in some city and people are going to lose access to their data. There will be many malware outbreaks, and many servers will crash today. Power surges, employee error (including file deletion and overwriting) will all happen today. Someone will click on a link in an email or web site and it will prove to be a link to malware. It is an odds game at the end of the day, but like the sun rising and setting, it is always going to happen. It is just a matter of when.

And since you cannot say with any assurance it cannot or will not happen to your organization, ask yourself how prepared you will be if the unthinkable happens?

According to a Gartner report, small-to-medium-sized businesses, let's say under 500 employees, will lose access to their data two times a year. It could be a physical malfunction, it could be a logical malfunction, or it could be fire or flood. Each time they lose access, they are down for an average of seven hours. For a small business with 50 employees, the hourly cost of down time is $9,000. If you extrapolate that, $9,000 times seven is $63,000 twice a year, so you are talking about $126,000 of down time related to loss of access to data, without considering loss of revenue. Still think you cannot afford to have a proper plan in place? I think you can.

The loss of revenue alone is frightening. For example, CPAs, architects, lawyers bill by the hour. If they cannot work, they cannot bill and those hours don't magically reappear.

What about sending out your accounts? Can businesses really afford to add a couple of extra days in receivables?

And what if, as part of a supply chain, your large

company is contractually obligated to produce your piece of that chain in minutes, hours, or days, and you can't produce due to a lack of access to your data? Get ready for some lawsuits.

Legally, many business and services are mandated to protect their data availability. Look at the changes happening with healthcare. Electronic Medical Records are required. You can't find a paper copy to save your life. There is no option not to have that electronic resource available to the professionals that need it when they need it.

Susan: So even when we don't think we have the money to spend on a proper data-protection plan, we probably can't afford not to have the right strategy in place. The cost is too high to gamble with data.

Domenic: Yes, that is 100% accurate. My biggest challenge is getting past the 'it will never happen to me' syndrome.

Susan: In today's day and age, customers don't have a lot of tolerance for downed websites. If your website goes down, we just go to the next company and order from their website. Versus, say, 15 years ago, when if a server goes down you're still taking phone calls and processing orders. That's not always the case anymore. Server crashes can mean no orders are being taken period.

Domenic: Very true, Susan. There is also a loss of reputation associated with a downed website. Companies lose business when their customers cannot connect to their website, especially when that website is their primary way of placing orders.

Additionally, when a company loses their client's data, that client loses trust and the company's reputation takes a hit. It's not fun to go to a client and tell them their data has been lost.

It has been said that making customers happy is harder than ever. Customers have the world at their fingertips 24/7 and maintaining customer loyalty means never being unavailable.

Why Disaster Can Strike at Any Businesses

Susan: How can a business make sure they are not accidentally overlooking a key component of their business continuity plan?

Domenic: First, let's clear up some of the different terminology. There is backup, business continuity, and disaster recovery. Backup is a subset of disaster recovery, which is a subset of business continuity.

My company is an IT consulting firm and we play mostly in the game of disaster recovery—that's disaster as it pertains to your IT infrastructure. Business continuity, which is the big brother of disaster recovery, also takes into consideration location, so where your work is going to go if your building burns down. Do we have a hot (meaning ready to go) colocation provisioned that allows people to connect remotely, when people cannot get to work?

There are many, many, many different aspects outside of the IT arena to consider. In this book, we're not talking about those components of disaster recovery. We are focusing on disaster recovery as it pertains to your computers and everything that they connect to including mobile devices.

Disaster recovery has become a central conversation these days, as businesses try to come up with a strategy for protecting their employees' data as well as the corporation's data and managing employees' ability to select locations (like phones and laptops) for their data that are not easily controlled by the business

We support a metal fabrication company, and they were hit with the Cryptolocker virus that I talked about earlier. The virus spreads insidiously because it not only affects your data and your file servers, but also any directories that are shared on your network.

It just so happened that a senior executive of this company lost a directory on his local hard drive, his C drive. It was some financial material. I was always cautioning him, reminding him that data on his local drive was not backed up and that it should be on the server so we would get it backed up. Two weeks later I got a terse call from the exec because he had a hard drive failure and he realized that his personal financials were gone and pictures of his grandkids that meant a lot to him. But also gone was an important business file that he had inadvertently saved to his C: drive rather than the company shared file.

At that point, I imagine, this guy started valuing his data. He was lucky, because when we took him on as a client, we had done backups of the workstations. We got most of his information back, but that does not always happen. I can guarantee that he started saving all his data changes to the file server from that day forward and realized that his personal information needed a backup strategy as well.

The old saying is applicable here, 'We protect what we value.' Do you really understand the value of your data? Most people do not until it is gone. In fact, here is a story to illustrate this very point.

From Our Blog…

Coffee, Tea or Business Continuity

Posted by Domenic DiSario on Sun, Sep 28, 2014 @ 07:09 PM

If the old saying "We protect what we value" is true, it seems I value my morning cup of coffee and my Internet access more than anything else in this world (family and friends excluded of course).

Why would I say this? Well, let me tell you a story.

We moved to North Andover, MA, about seven years ago, just inside Harold Parker State Forest. It's a beautiful spot to live, but we discovered very soon after we moved that even a very moderate wind can knock out the power. And lose power we did! About 10 times in the last seven years. First time was traumatic, being the city folk that we were. But we learned. We got a generator, made sure there was plenty of propane, and got a DC converter for the car. Losing power continues to be a huge inconvenience, but we are pretty much prepared these days.

About a month ago, I was sitting in my chair browsing the Internet while drinking my morning coffee. We had lost power the night before, and we were running on a generator. And although a little inconvenienced, I was relatively content.

As I thought about how comfortable I was I realized I had built in three layers of fault tolerance to make sure I got my morning coffee, could check my email, and perform other Internet-related tasks no matter what.

For coffee, I had the generator as a primary source. If that failed, I could always turn on the car, plug in the DC/AC converter, throw an extension cord out the window, plug it all in, and brew the coffee. I also had the gas grill where I could boil some water and use our french press system.

For Internet, I had the generator, which works fine if the outage is local. But if it is regional and the Comcast facility is down, I always have my good old Verizon 4G Card or the Hotspot on my iPhone.

So, there I was with multiple layers of fault tolerance for my coffee and two layers for my Internet access, which, as it turned out, was more layers of fault tolerance than I had for my company file servers and infrastructure. As the owner of a computer support company, this was both surprising and unacceptable.

Do I value my cup of coffee more than my company data?

Maybe I need my coffee more than my data at that moment?

Whatever the case, it was a wakeup call at my company. We now have at least as many layers of fault tolerance for our servers and other critical equipment as I do for my morning coffee.

What is your strategy? Do you have your head in the sand hoping for the best? Do you really know what your data is worth and what downtime could possibly cost you?

- Fire
- Flood
- Natural Disaster
- Man-made Disaster
- Virus Outbreak (Remember CryptoLocker)

All of the above have happened at some point recently. Maybe not to all of us. At least not yet.

This is truly a numbers game, and you never know. And besides: Hope is not a strategy.

For more information, visit:
http://backupfanatic.com

How to Protect Your Business from a Disaster

Susan: How can businesses like the one you describe protect themselves from a disaster? What do they need to know, Domenic?

Domenic: The first thing they must do is accept the need for data protection as a business necessity. The second thing they need to understand is the ramifications of data loss. What happens if their server crashes, and I cannot recover the data?

I try to take them through that scenario because the majority of businesses I support do in fact have some type of backup. The problem is that it is often inadequate, and they get a false sense of security. I ask when I go in, "What are you doing for backup?" "Oh, we back it up to tape," which is astonishing. When you think backup tape, you think IBM 1968, right?

Susan: Right.

Domenic: In middle-sized and larger businesses, 52% still use tape, which is frightening because tapes are susceptible to heat, to humidity, to magnetic fields. Every tape will fail eventually. Statistically recoveries from tapes are less than 50% successful. Businesses believe they are backing up their data, but their sense of security is false. They also have zero assurance they'll be able to <u>access</u> the data on those tapes.

They must know *what* they need to back up and *where* it is. Hopefully, all their data is on their file servers, but this is usually not the case. As I've noted, I run into the renegade, "Oh, this is too personal. I'm putting it on my local drive." So during our review of their strategy we talk a lot about simple administrative procedures for file locations and naming conventions and that type of thing.

But here is the most important point: a simple backup is not enough. Even if we are backing up everything, backup without recovery is useless. I could be backing up all day long, but if I cannot get it back, then the backup is literally useless.

From our Blog...

The Importance of Reliable Data Recovery (White Paper)

Most people don't understand how important recovery is. When I ask about data backup, people usually say they backup on a tape or an external hard drive or the cloud.

Then I take them through a recovery scenario, and things get more complicated. Most people – I'd say 99% – back up their data once a night. Maybe the other one percent backup a couple of times a day, never more than that (unless, of course, you are one of my clients). So they back up once or twice a day, and they are getting it all, so I take them to the next step.

So, now, all your data is on the server. We have determined that through this conversation. What happens if that server crashes? What happens if the power supply goes, the motherboard fries, or it gets infected by some malware, and it is inoperable? What's next?

Well, you'll need a new server. So even if you are getting a total backup of your data, if you need a new server for whatever reason, the first thing you need to do is secure a new server. How long is that going to take? Maybe a day, maybe two days, maybe three days? Let's go best case scenario: let's say that they had an extra server in the house, right? Very unusual, but I am trying to make a point. So let's say I have a spare server in the closet.

Alright now let's pull that server out and plug it in. I get the data back easily enough, but in order for the data to be useful, there are steps. I have to get the server plugged in, get it powered up, and I have to install an operating system. The Windows server operating system might take four hours to install, and I am being very liberal about these times. Usually it is longer.

But what about all their applications? The chances of having the CD is slim to none, but let's assume they have it all in a nice little cabinet or on the shelf. Now I have to install the QuickBooks, the Peachtree, the line-of-business apps, the Microsoft Office, whatever it is. There are going to be, on average, a dozen applications that every company uses.

Now I have to find all the software, install it, and patch it up for the latest version. That is at least another four hours, and again I'm being very liberal. This could be 20 times longer than that.

We've already spent eight hours and are just at the point where we can finally restore our data. If it is a significant amount of local data, we are talking at least another two, three, or four hours. If it is in the cloud, we are talking days or weeks, so forget it.

This is why, when we talk about business continuity strategies and solutions, we always need to include a local copy of your data just for this scenario because you need to restore it in a timely manner.

Backup, Disaster Recovery and Business Continuity for the SMB (White Paper)

What we should be looking for an a solution:

- Is designed to reduce any server down time to 30 minutes.

- Allows near real-time backups as frequent as every 15 minutes.

- Includes offsite backup.

- Provides a simple and efficient recovery process.

- Encryption so data it is not accessible to anyone, either locally or at the remote storage facility without the passkey.

- Eliminates the cost and time of managing on-site tape backup. Automatically monitored and maintained.

- All inclusive solution (on site backups, on site virtual server, remote storage, disaster recovery in the event of disaster and 24x7 management of the entire process are bundled at a price that is comparable to the overall cost of buying and managing tape backup.)

Executive Summary

A recent study discovered that, of companies experiencing a "major loss" of computer records, 43 percent never reopened, 51 percent closed within two years of the loss, and a mere 6 percent survived over the long-term. For small and medium-sized businesses (SMB's) in particular, these statistics suggest the necessity of crafting a business continuity strategy grounded in a robust data backup and recovery solution.

Unlike enterprises, many smaller companies cannot afford optimal in-house disaster recovery strategies. These companies are consequently at an elevated risk of being put out of business due to any major loss of data. Loss of data could mean emails lost, accounting data lost, patient or client files lost, company records lost, client legal records or orders lost and so on. This white paper evaluates the scope of disaster recovery and business continuity for smaller companies, by examining their challenges. We'll also discuss how our solution overcomes commonly-faced challenges to offer the most comprehensive solution out in the marketplace.

IT Disaster Recovery Planning for Small and Medium Size Businesses

A DR Plan is the blueprint for how businesses plan to survive everything from local equipment failure to global disaster. Data-oriented DR Planning, an indispensable component of business planning regardless of organization size, poses the following challenges. Smaller businesses generally lack the in-house IT resources to achieve these demanding planning, technical and process requirements. Therefore, many SMBs either neglect to implement any data-oriented business continuity plan or else approach data backup and recovery in a sporadic, rudimentary fashion that fails to conform to the best practices of DR and Business Continuity Planning.

Understanding the risks of not having a plan in place

- Understanding regulatory compliance requirements in your industry. Regulations such as the Healthcare Insurance Portability and Accountability Act (HIPAA) and the Gramm-Leach-Bliley Act (GLBA) and other laws- state and federal mandates.

- Understanding how to mitigate the risk of losing vital business data, such as customer records.

- Being aware of the environmental hazards that the business infrastructure is exposed to due to your geographical location.

- Estimating time it would take to build the business back if disaster strikes without having any DR planning in place.

- Understanding ROI for having a plan in place.

- Identifying the lowest-cost, highest-performance data backup medium (tape or disk) based solution and keeping abreast with the latest and greatest in the industry.

- Ensure that all backed-up data is encrypted and otherwise safeguarded from theft.

- Ensure that backed-up data can be restored

to different kinds of hardware.

- Ensure that data backup continues even during active recovery phases.

Operational Challenges

- Identifying what data to back up.

- Identifying how frequently to back up and related costs and ROI.

- Retain the ability to recover not only the most recent data, but also data from older time horizons, such as past quarters and years.

- Retain the ability to monitor and manage the integrity of ongoing data backup processes so that backup failures can be diagnosed and remedied before adversely impacting the DR lifecycle.

- The need to hire staff who can understand, design, implement and manage a system to get business back in action quickly after disaster strikes.

Traditional Solution vs. Current Solutions

Implementing a data-oriented DR strategy first requires designation of a specific data storage medium. Magnetic tape and disks are the two leading media for data backup storage. While magnetic tape is currently dominant, analyst Dave Russell of Gartner believes that "recovery will move to online disk-based storage in the future. This will cause a major shift in the backup market during the next four to five years."

Smaller companies in particular will benefit from the shift, as recent advances in design and manufacturing lower the total cost of disk-based storage in terms of storage per bit. Falling prices, combined with the various performance advantages that storage industry analysts cite, render disk increasingly attractive. Gartner Group highlights the suitability of disk for these organizations by explaining that, "the need for high-performance online recovery of data, combined with the availability of low-cost disk arrays, has influenced enterprises and small and midsize businesses to adopt a disk-based approach for backup and recovery."

Tape, in contrast to disk, is physically delicate and easily compromised by environmental factors such as heat, humidity, and magnetic interference. Moreover, tape cartridges must be replaced frequently (every 6-12 months). Tape's innate sensitivity contributes to high failure rates, with analysts estimating that anywhere from 42 to 71 percent of tape restores fail. Even when magnetic tape backups are successful, tapes themselves are subject to loss or theft, and may be in the possession of an employee or vendor unable to reach a recovery site. Thus, even when physical backup and restoration processes succeed, tape may not prove to be as timely and appropriate a medium for data storage as disk. Time is a crucial consideration because each hour of server, application, and network downtime endured until data restoration comes at a high cost, especially to smaller businesses.

Analyst Jon Oltsik of Enterprise Strategy Group also points out that tape is seldom encrypted, compounding the destructive impact of tape theft: "Very few people encrypt backup tapes, which means that they rely on the security of the backup and off-site rotation process."

Disk offers not only lower-cost encryption but also other advantages. In contrast to tape, "disks are more durable, last longer, withstand more overwriting and you don't need to clean any heads," according to Rinku Tyagi of PCQuest. Additionally, "When it comes to backing up using disks, they are easier to manage. Disk backup systems include management tools, often browser-based, for you to easily configure settings and check status from anywhere."

HP enumerates other advantages of disk storage, noting that "data is backed up to disk much faster than tape, which translates to less impact on production server availability. Disk is also a more reliable media than tape and less prone to error, which translates to less failed recoveries".

While disk offers advantages over tape, it is not a panacea. After installing disk technology, companies will still be responsible for monitoring and managing backup processes, encrypting and safeguarding backed-up onsite and offsite data, restoring data to new hardware, and other functions. Without implementing a layer of governance over disk-based data backup, these companies court the danger of failed backups and delayed restoration of data, thereby jeopardizing their chances of successful recovery from major data loss.

Smaller companies unable or unwilling to invest in the human expertise and infrastructure support systems necessary for data-oriented DR Plan can leverage our data backup and recovery solution, which removes cost and complexity burdens from your staff.

A Complete Solution that addresses all of your DR and BC Needs

Near Real-Time Backups: Various incremental methodology captures all changes to the initial image in increments of 15 minutes. These technologies not only back up recent datasets but also allow end users to reconstruct the state of their data as it stood at the end of various 15-minute restoration points. This level of forensic and auditable data recovery may satisfy various regulatory requirements (such as HIPAA and GLBA and various State and Federal requirements) for data retention and data record reconstruction, and also serves stakeholders such as supply chain planners, warehouse analysts, auditors, and legal counsel.

On-site and Cloud-Based Virtual Servers

If any of your servers fail, our server virtualization technology embedded in the Network Attached Storage (NAS) allows customer servers and applications to be restored and rebooted in less than 30 minutes in most cases. As you may sometimes endure a wait of several days in order to receive replacement servers from vendors, your NAS can have your business up and running. The NAS multitasks so that, even while functioning as a virtual server, it can continue to back up data from other devices plugged into the NAS. Our technology thus allows you to remain in business without any significant loss of data backup, server functionality, or application downtime. In the event of a site disaster, we can spin up all of your servers in our Cloud facilities.

A Complete Image at various time points

We generate an image of all hard drive partitions via an agent, which is warehoused on the NAS device physically located at your site. The data is stored using AES-256 encryption and compressed. We employ a block-level, not file-level, backup, which means that data is captured at the level of 1's and 0's. Block level data is raw data which does not have a file structure imposed on it. Database applications such as Microsoft SQL Server and Microsoft Exchange Server transfer data in blocks. Block transfer is the most efficient way to write to disk and is much less prone to errors such as those that result from file-level backups. Additionally, block level backups are not affected by open files or open databases. The block-level image is an exact digital duplicate of the on-site server.

Intuitive and Flexible Restore Options

A good backup system should allow for quick and flexible restores. Our solution allows for recovery of files, folders, partitions, mailboxes/messages, and databases/tables using a quick and intuitive process. In case of a complete server failure, we do support a bare metal restore to new hardware which has a different configuration, hardware and drivers as compared to the failed server. Our 15-minute incremental based backup allows restores to be done from any point in time, allowing for multiple versions of files, folders, messages/mailboxes, and database/tables to be restored.

Secure Off-Site Storage

After imaging the servers to which it is attached, the NAS device then creates an independent 256-bit encrypted tunnel and transmits the imaged data to a secure offsite location where it resides in an encrypted, compressed format. That remote site then replicates again to an alternate data center, creating a total of three copies of the data in three geographically distinct regions. Since the data is encrypted and only you have the key, no one has access at any of the remote storage facilities.

Transmitting data to a remote site is a key component of DR and business continuity. It guarantees that, in case of physical damage to the client's network or NAS, or even regional disaster, the data is safe in uncompromised locations. Encryption is an important step in the process of transmitting data between the NAS and the remote sites, because it greatly reduces the risk of data loss incidents that plague magnetic tape and prevents man-in-the-middle attacks during transmission. We employ the 256-bit Advanced Encryption Standard (AES) algorithm because it has never been broken and is currently considered the gold standard of encryption techniques and renders transmitted data immune to theft.

Secure, Bandwidth Throttling Transfer

Transmission itself occurs over your Internet connection, and can easily be configured to minimize bandwidth consumption. Our NAS leverages Adaptive Bandwidth Throttling, which only utilizes unused bandwidth or allows us to set an outbound limit. Our UDP based smart transfer technology utilizes a host of innovative algorithms to speed up data transport and resume from failure. We can therefore exercise fine control over the data imaging and transmission processes.

24x7 Completely Managed Solution

Network Operations Center (NOC) monitors your NAS units and the attached servers 24/7. Failed processes generate immediate alerts to our engineers, who often remotely correct errors within minutes of receiving notification. In case of more serious NAS issues, we will conduct repairs at your site. If any NAS units are irreparably damaged or destroyed, at an additional cost we will overnight replacements pre-loaded with all stored data directly to your location.

Affordable Cost

Look for a pricing package that is inclusive of the complete backup and disaster recovery service- with no hidden costs. All your costs are bundled and include the NAS, the Incremental Forever Methodology, file restorations, file integrity checks, secure data transmission and remote storage.

**For more information, visit:
http://backupfanatic.com**

Back to the Interview….

Susan: Are you saying when you back up in the cloud it could literally take a business weeks to get their data restored?

Domenic: Yes, because you are depending on an Internet connection, which is one one-thousandth as fast as the local connection. That is an average, and not an exaggeration or worst case scenario by any stretch.

Let's assume for the sake of argument that they do have a local copy of their data. It is going to take us an additional four hours to get that data back. Now they have been down 12 hours—a day and a half of work. I tell the business owner, "Best case, you are down 12 hours, are you okay with that?" Then I show them the loss of profitability due to downtime; no one is okay with that.

What I just described, Susan, is called RTO—Recovery Time Objective. Companies need to ask themselves, "What are our objectives and how quickly do we want to be back up?" Usually people say, "I can go half a day, maybe a day." Some people kid themselves and say, "I can go three days, but…" Then the question is how long do you want to take to recover the data. That's the Recovery Time Objective, which in my opinion should be in minutes, much less than an hour.

But let's talk about another part of this that maybe isn't so obvious.

You got all your data back, but when was the data last backed up? This is called the RPO—Recovery Point Objective. Because there is so much data, it usually takes companies eight to 12 hours to perform a full backup. This creates such a long backup window that most companies only back up once a day.

Say they back up at 10:00 at night. Now let's say at 1:00 pm the next day their server crashes, and they need to do a recovery. That would mean they lost a whole morning, and any data point important to any of their systems is now gone, period.

People do not understand this, and they tend to be overly optimistic about how much data they can live without. Even if they are correct in their assumptions, some companies governed by various compliance standards have no choice but to live within these strict standards or they could be faced with heavy fines and penalties.

In short, companies need to know how much data they have, if it is being backed up, and if it can be recovered in a complete and timely manner. The answer is often they just don't know. They do not know how much data they have. They do not know where it is, and they do not know if it can be recovered in a timely manner.

How to Protect Your Personal Data in the Event of a Disaster

Susan: Can you talk to us about what to do when you work remotely? How can you stay protected then? A lot of people are very mobile; they work from home, but not all the time, and they travel with their laptops. What do you recommend in that scenario?

Domenic: Trying to manage the situation you describe is a real challenge for companies these days. And it's not just about protecting the data they lose invariably on these devices because they are not performing local backup on their system nor is their data being transferred to the companies' main servers for companywide backup.

There's a local copy of the last couple of months' worth of emails on my iPhone. From a data protection point of view, in this particular case, the email is not a big deal, right? If I lose my iPhone, I buy a new one, re-sync it, and I'm good. But what about from a security point of view?

What if those emails on my phone have protected information, and I'm in danger of violating various state and federal privacy regulations? Some regulations state if you have any two pieces of information, a social security number, bank account, first name, last name, insurance number then that combination of data needs to be protected and encrypted.

If you are HIPAA regulated and you lose your phone, and you know that there were emails on that phone with protected information and the phone wasn't encrypted and locked, you are legally obligated to turn yourself in. And if you don't turn yourself in, I'm legally obligated to turn you in.

Data on mobile devices is a big deal because it is mobile, and therefore can be lost easily. It is estimated that one out of every 10 laptops is going to be stolen. The problem is one of comprehension. Sometimes laptop owners do not seem to understand they have company information on their local drive.

Or maybe they do understand, and they're just not careful. They copy to their laptop the three spreadsheets they want to work on over the weekend, and then their laptop is stolen. Or, maybe worse than that, they work the whole weekend and their laptop is stolen on Sunday night. So not only is there a possible data breach, but all that work they did is gone because they did not upload their modified sheets to the server.

There are a lot of data backup and malware considerations with mobile computing, which makes encryption a very big thing. I could lose this phone with 1,000 HIPAA regulated records, and if it is encrypted, I do not even have to report it. But if I had one piece of HIPAA protected information on it that was not encrypted, I'd have to report it as a data breach.

Not only are mobile devices easy to lose—they're also easy to break.

These devices need to be backed up and protected from physical damage, which is much overlooked. Even when people have a great disaster recovery/business continuity plan in place, and they're backing up all their servers, which they can recover within five minutes not only locally but also in a replicated version in the cloud, the physical workstations, phones, and tablets are often overlooked. And if there is unique data on those devices, the bottom line is, it's gone. It does not matter how much you back up the server; if the information is only on the phone, you lose it.

From our Blog…

State wide regulations sometimes are more rigorous than federal regulations. For Example Massachusetts Privacy Regulations - A not so gentle reminder: they exist and they have teeth!

"BSU can prevent Technology Separation Anxiety"

It's a little over four years since the MA Privacy Regulations 201 CMR 17:00 went into law.

Here are four questions to ask yourself:

1) Are you compliant?

2) Do you have a WISP? Have you reviewed it recently? Can you locate it?

3) Do you execute the yearly and other event-driven requirement actions?

4) Do you even remember there is such a law?

I work for a company of IT consultants, and I shudder to think about various security holes we find when doing network and security assessments for potential clients. With tax season just about to end, I wonder how may unencrypted emails were sent out containing personal information?

Penalties for Mass. Personal Information Law Violation - 201 CMR 17.00

- Up to $50,000 per improper disposal.

- Maximum of $5,000 per violation.

- Above penalties don't include lost business, dealing with irate customers, mailing out letters, and other associated costs.

- Courts can order treble the damages if it's concluded that there was a willful or knowing violation.

According to the **Chief of Consumer Protection Division, MA Attorney General's Office,** the AG's Office is looking for warning signals that may indicate noncompliance with the regulations that would trigger a detailed investigation. Some of the circumstances likely to trigger a detailed investigation include:

- The reporting entity knew of the breach, but failed to notify affected individuals as required by the Notice Law.

- A Written Information Security Plan (WISP) cannot be produced.

- The WISP is inadequate, or had significant gaps because of a lack of due diligence in the risk assessment process.

- The compromised data was stored or maintained in circumstances not compliant with the "reasonable" security required by the regulations.

- Unfairness or deception around the purpose for which the data was originally collected.

- Collected data that was subsequently used for purposes not disclosed to consumers, or where the collection itself is not disclosed leading to unfairness or deception to Massachusetts residents.

With the proliferation of BYOD (Bring Your Own Device), employees are using smartphones and tablets in the workplace more and more, which exponentially increases the risks as well as the ramifications of improperly protecting personal information (PI). The likelihood of Private Information being present on these devices is extremely high. An lost or stolen unencrypted device (or one without PIN protection) that contains PI calls for immediate notification to the proper agencies and is considered a breach. If, however, the device was encrypted and PIN protected, it would not be considered a breach even if it contained thousands of records of PI. In summary, encryption and PIN protection equals "Safe harbor."

For more information, visit: http://backupfanatic.com

Back to the interview...

Domenic: You have heard of BYOD—Bring Your Own Device. Many companies are adopting that policy where they let people bring their own devices to work. It makes sense because as the workforce changes, people's device of choice changes. A lot of young people would rather work on a tablet. Even a generation younger, they're going to be working on a phone and texting as a matter of course, so companies have a difficult time managing these devices and often just ignore them all together.

BYOD might be less expensive for companies because they are not supplying a device for their employees. But I would argue that correctly managing those devices is exponentially more expensive than just supplying a laptop, and here's why: you cannot enforce company policies on a personal device.

I can give you an example. If I have both business and personal information on my personal phone, and I lose it, even if the company has the capability to remotely wipe that phone clean, it's illegal unless you have a way to segregate the data. In other words, I can wipe the business data, but I have to leave that person's personal data intact, so it becomes a management nightmare.

Fortunately, there is something called MDM—or, Mobile Device Management—, which has been available for a couple of years. In essence, it allows you to do what I just said: segregate the different types of data, so you can blow up some data, but leave the pictures of the grandkids alone.

From our Blog...

MDM for the SMB: a must!

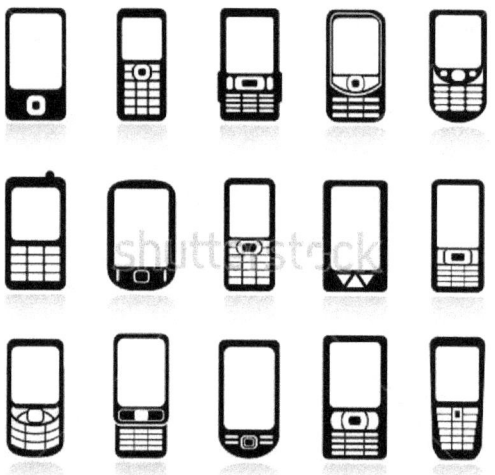

As more workers use mobile devices to complete an ever-expanding multitude of job-related processes and tasks, managing them becomes increasingly complex and more necessary. Enter Mobile Device Management or MDM. Mobile device management (MDM) platforms are available for use in firms of all sizes. Their utility lies in administering real time mobility policies throughout the enterprise, assuring expanded employee connectivity for the growing use of mobile devices, such as tablets and deep-utility smartphones. The increasing need for employee connectivity brings with it serious security issues, as well as a need to revise enterprise data-access procedures and assure the SMB's data is protected on all fronts. MDM should be implemented in all businesses including the SMB to provide appropriate administration and protection of these devices, and to maintain an operational/competitive parity with larger firms.

As with larger firms, mobile policy for SMBs focuses on the provisioning of fluid and secure data access from disparate locations. Simple messaging platforms no longer suffice. Increased use of rich media management through adoption of MDM policies and platforms is essential for the SMB to maintain a competitive standing. The question is, how do you secure and manage these mobile devices? The answer of course is Mobile Device Management (MDM). MDM will become more important as enterprise applications for mobile encompass most business transactions and related communication. Among these are data input, employee recruitment, record-keeping, customer communications, and financial management. Unique mobile-apps will distinguish a firm from its rivals, generating competitive advantage and opportunity to expand market share and revenues through flexible, real-time performance; they all require MDM for best-use implementation.

However, specialized apps will require a finer degree of MDM supervision to provide quality business performance, without compromising the SMB's enterprise strategies and objectives. Maintaining multiple mobile platforms produces scrupulous quality assurance (QA) for measuring real-world performance and infrastructure adaptability. Best-practice MDM establishes the SMB's policies for deploying mobile workflows, as well as those administrative, budgetary and security practices best-suited to the firm, supervising performance and QA, without compromising enterprise needs or breaking the bank.

For SMBs, where the security issues of BYOD, potential data loss or leakage, are more serious, implementing digital asset management (DAM) is suggested for supervising, chronicling and distributing information to mobile workers. MDM improves monitoring of workers' mobile operating systems and resource-management; network surveillance also improves. Though all these functions are built for enterprise mobile, the issue of security always requires adroit management.

MDM security for SMBs must conscientiously monitor mobile operations to generate best-practice protection, particularly with the increasing emphasis on Cloud apps among mobile users and the firms they work for. Cloud's ease of use, flexibility and speed of operation sometimes mask heightened security issues, chiefly in the form of disrupted transmission or modified content from off-premise sources. Tablets are exceptionally valuable and are becoming as popular as smartphones for corporate mobile; however their encryption/security apps require constant monitoring when in use and additional development to improve protection of SMB corporate information. These measures of security remain pressing concerns for the SMB.

There is some agreement among SMB executives that workplace mobility will continue to proliferate and perhaps dominate business operations. Nevertheless, many SMBs remain unfamiliar with MDM, despite the fact most use at least some form of mobile computing for work purposes.

Mobile devices increasingly replace desktop and laptop computers, even in on-premise situations. A large-scale bring-your-own-device (BYOD) conversion, where employees use their own mobile devices for work purposes, is well upon us, even where firms may supply their workers with mobility options. Under these circumstances, MDM assumes greater significance; a well-conceived mobile policy — focusing on functions like application/device supervision and wireless provisioning, as well as security — is recommended for all SMBs seeking to remain competitive in the future.

For more information, visit: http://backupfanatic.com

How Old Technology Can Expose You to Risk

Susan: What else do companies need to know about keeping their data safe?

Domenic: Here's another point companies should consider: there are a lot of Windows 2003 servers in existence within organizations currently. Microsoft will stop supporting these servers, as well as Windows XP desktops, in July of 2015 .

When Microsoft stops supporting older technology, Microsoft stops producing security patches for these devices. Needless to say, this raises the risk of exposure in an organization. Microsoft is no longer patching and closing the holes created by the known bugs in these old operating systems. Additionally, virus and malware protection companies like Norton, McAfee's, and ESET have ceased releasing updated virus signatures, so now these systems are susceptible to the latest viruses and malware.

In essence, there are still many 2003 servers out there with nothing new being done to protect them. Every day I can't upgrade a virus signature file for that server means one more virus that I'm not protected against. We talked about Cryptolocker, which is going to lock up many of your systems files. Identity theft is also huge. Hackers just put a piece of malware on your system and they can see your every keystroke.

A couple of weeks ago, 60 Minutes did a story on identity theft during Christmas time. They interviewed many of the big chain stores like Walmart, and they said that 90% of the systems have been infiltrated.

There are many ways to lose data. It's about more than a server crashing or someone deleting a file. Your data also can be affected by malware, which renders it unusable. And using unsupported software is a bad idea. These days, more often than not, you are going to see more malware infections than server crashes by far.

Pay attention also to how your employees access the internet. There are plenty of YouTube embedded viruses that will cripple your systems. You may have a program that controls access to social media at work. That will do you no good when an employee using a laptop brings that virus to work. Rigorous malware scanning and patching are critical.

From our Blog…

Are you ready for the end of service for Windows Server 2003?

July 2015 will mark the end of Windows Server 2003 Extended Support. What does that mean for current Server 2003 owners? It means Microsoft will no longer release new security patches or updates, putting your whole business at risk from new viruses and potential performance problems due to incompatibilities with newer software and applications.

If your business still uses Windows Server 2003 you will need a plan and you will need it soon. Analysts are estimating that approximately 10 million machines are still running Windows Server 2003. These machines will soon be without support from Microsoft. This issue will especially affect regulated industries such as healthcare and financial as they will need to maintain the security and confidentiality of these outdated and unsupported servers.

It is extremely important to consider how this new information will affect your business. Here are few factors:

Cost

With the end of service to Windows Server 2003, the cost of required tools to keep your systems online, such as intrusion detection systems, more advanced firewalls, etc. makes buying Windows Server 2012 a less expensive alternative.

Security

The end of service will put your business at risk, since there will be no fixes for bugs and viruses or patches for system vulnerabilities.

Compliance

Certain professions require regular audits to fulfill regulation requirements. Mounting compliance expenses as well as the price of audits will make the upgrade to Windows Server 2012 another less *expensive alternative.*

What are your options?

The only option available right now is to migrate your data from Windows Server 2003 to Windows Server 2012. The migration must be performed by professionals in order to ensure the safety of your data, especially considering this migration will involve a move between 32-bit and 64-bit platforms.

In summary, it is important to look ahead and ensure that you take steps to protect your business well ahead of the July 2015 deadline.

For more information, visit:
http://backupfanatic.com

Proof Disaster Can Strike Twice

Susan: Can you share with us some examples of companies where disaster struck? What were the results?

Domenic: Sure. This first story happened 10 years ago, so it goes to show that this is not a brand new problem. This problem has been around for a long time, but the exponential growth of data to store has made it even worse.

I have more data in my pocket than I had in a file server for a 300-person company five years ago. In 1980, it cost a half million dollars per gigabyte of storage because in the 1980s, we were measuring in kilobytes and megabytes. A gigabyte of data was considered a lot of data. Today a gigabyte of data is not, in the scheme of things today, considered a lot of data. You can buy a gigabyte of storage for a ten cents, and you can buy a terabyte, 1000 times a gigabyte for less than $100. People are unaware of the amount of data that they do store since storing it is cheap. When time comes to restore the data, they are astonished at the time it takes to do it.

This first story happened at a defense contractor in New Hampshire. We were the consultants. The company had many locations and a full IT staff. This wasn't a billion dollar company, but they had just spent tens of thousands of dollars on a backup solution, which they were very confident about.

Every morning, they would get an email with the logs, which stated their backup was 100%

complete. As we already discussed, a backup without recovery is useless. So a big part of any business continuity plan should constitute regular tests to make sure that those backups are actually happening and the data is recoverable. In this particular case, they were not doing their monthly tests and, when their server crashed, it turned out their tape-based backup system did not work.

The log indicated a 100% complete backup, but there was nothing on the tape. In fact, after they escorted the IT manager out the door (that was his last day there), it took us weeks to recover what we could. They were designing systems and software for the government, so I estimate they lost millions of dollars worth of data.

The moral to that story is, it's great to have a backup. It is great to look at those logs, but without a test restore on a regular basis, I know I am not comfortable. Also, relying on a medium as flawed as tape is not wise. Any one single solution is inherently risky.

Another example started with a call I got this time last year: "Please come to my company, we have an emergency." So I drove over to the company but when I went to the front door, I could not get in because they had this large plotter blocking the door.

This is an architectural firm, and you know what a plotter looks like? They are about four feet long. It is where they print all the architectural plans. This plotter was jammed in the door because someone was trying to steal it. They didn't end up getting the plotter, but they did manage to get their mail server through the door. I am sure that was not their goal. I am sure they did not understand how valuable that data was. They probably resold the server on eBay for $300, but this company lost their file server and therefore all their data through a theft.

This architectural firm lost all of their email because when they went to recover from backup, their data was simply not there.

In the end, they were very fortunate. They did get a a lot of email back because they were using active sync, which is the mechanism that allows you to see emails on phones. This allowed us to re-sync the phones back to the new mail server.

If you want an idea of how much data is worth, this will give you some perspective. This company got $300,000 from their insurance company for the data they lost, which, again, was not a complete loss because we got a lot of it back by syncing the phones back into the server.

In another company we were called in because their last IT company, when a crisis arose they simply could not recover the data when they needed to.

This company lost weeks worth of information, but their records were mirrored partly on paper and they were small enough to be able to rebuild from those records. They're not out of business yet, but industry data is clear. Of companies who lose a substantial amount of their data, fifty percent never re-open their doors or, if they do, they're out of business within a year.

The same company did learn from this experience and did have our continuity system in place when one of their servers crashed. It was 10PM. We spun up the replicated version of their server in the cloud by 11PM. When their users came in the next morning, they did not even know the server was gone. When their new server was ready and in place, we simply shut them down again at 10:00 at night and copied the cloud version back down to their device. In the morning, we just imaged it back to their server, and they did not lose more than a half hour of effective work time.

On at least a weekly basis I get a call, "I accidentally deleted this email folder, or deleted this message, this directory's gone, where is it?" Because of our diligence, we are always able to recover a very recent copy. Be certain your IT support considers business continuity to be of the highest priority.

Here Are the Mistakes to Avoid When Doing Your Disaster Recovery

Susan: What are some of the mistakes you have seen people make when it comes to their disaster recovery?

Domenic: One of the messages of this book is *Intelligent Business Continuity*, 'Intelligent' being the operative word. First, they do not know where their critical data is. They really do not. When I ask a business owner, "Where is your critical data located?" they often reply, "I don't know. My IT person has it covered."

Now I don't expect business owners to know the technical aspects of their network and business systems but I do expect that they will set the policies for business continuity data and will know the basics of their IT structure including documentation of their system and proof that their IT support (in-house or outsourced) uses best practices to keep the business running.

The biggest mistake I see is not understanding recovery mechanisms. Even if you know where your data is, even if you have it all backed up, and even if you have done test recoveries and you know that data is good, you still have two problems. The first problem is how quickly you can get it back. The second problem is the RPO, Recovery Point Objective. How recent is the data? Did you lose a half a day? Did you lose a day? Did you lose three hours? What is acceptable?

It does not matter what the answer is, the question

is, is that okay? The biggest mistake in this process is not understanding that even if your data can successfully be restored, can you do it without downtime? Can the restore be done at night? Can users still work during recovery?

I have to say that people just do not want to hear these questions. They just want to believe that they are okay and if they do have a disaster, somehow miraculously it is going to be resolved. This is ludicrous, but it happens. I see it all the time. It is like me thinking, "Oh, my house is going to be destroyed, but we will be all right because somehow it is going to be rebuilt tomorrow and I am going to be able to sleep in our bed tomorrow night."

That type of thinking, magical thinking, is no way to run a business.

Susan: That is actually a great analogy. I think a lot of people have home owner's insurance and think, if their house burns down, they will get a check and it will just fix the problem. But it does not.

Domenic: No, eventually you'll get your house rebuilt, but not the next day. Business continuity planning and implementation can certainly be less painful than rebuilding a house. But there are similar considerations.

We are a small company and support 100 or so companies, but I can guarantee you that within the next three months, one of those companies will have a server down. If they're using our business continuity product, they will be up immediately. If they are not, it is going to be painful and expensive for them and painful for me, too, because it is never pleasant trying to piecemeal something back together that you know is never going to be complete.

Frequently Asked Questions (FAQs)

1. What's the difference between business continuity planning and disaster recovery planning?

Business continuity typically pertains to the whole business, while disaster recovery includes only the IT-related components of the business. Both are critical to your business.

2. What is the purpose of having a business continuity plan?

The purpose of a business continuity plan is to try and assure an orderly and complete restoration of key business processes in the event of a business disruption.

3. Do I need IT business continuity if I already have a backup system?

The function of a backup system is to back up your data. That is only a small part of getting your business operational after a disaster.

4. What's the difference between cloud backup and cloud computing?

A cloud backup refers to a backup system in which you have a copy of your data offsite at a

data center. Cloud computing is when you have all of your resources (including your data) located in a data center, and you run them from there.

5. Do I need both disaster recovery and business continuity plan? If yes, then why?

Yes. A disaster recovery plan is only a small part of your business continuity plan. There are other parts needed to get your business back online subsequent to a disaster.

6. What's the difference between online backup, cloud backup, and online storage?

Online backup and cloud backup are the same thing. Online storage, on the other hand, means your cloud data is live and being worked on regularly (as opposed to just backup data).

7. How can I be sure that the cloud service provider will not lose my backed-up data? For example, what happens if the data storage server is destroyed or stolen?

All data centers worth considering have fault tolerance built in. Some things to look for are:

100% SLA Uptime Guarantee

Geographically dispersed redundant sites

SSAE16, HIPAA, PCI DSS, SOC 1&2 and Safe Harbor Compliant

Biometric Authentication

Fire Suppression

Full (N+1) Power with UPS Backup

Carrier Neutral

Above FEMA 500 Year Flood Plain

8. While using the services of cloud providers, can I really recover my critical systems within a very short time in the event of a disaster?

Assuming you are careful in choosing your provider, then definitely yes. Some solutions guarantee you'll be back up within an hour. Needless to say, regular testing of subsets of your recovery are mandatory if you want to be assured of this rapid recovery. Complete recovery fire drill recovery should also be done on a regular (but less frequent) basis.

9. What do RTO and RPO mean?

RTO stands for Recovery Time Objective and RPO stands for Recovery Point Objective. RTO is how long can you afford to be down and RPO is how much data can you afford to lose.

10. What are the advantages of local backup with the business continuity service?

Having a local copy of your backup data expedites the recovery process because access to the data and the restoration of the data (if need be) is much faster over local network connections than over the Internet. This

assumes, of course, that your local data did not get lost in the disaster. Local backups are most often used in partial disasters like server crashes and the like.

11. Who should do business continuity planning?

Everyone. Seriously, if your business cannot afford substantial downtime then disaster recovery and business continuity planning are mandatory.

Should Ask Questions (SAQs)

1. What's the difference between using backup software and copying?

Copying is a form of backup, I suppose, but without any of the management functions of backup software. With backup software, you can do various types of backups (e.g., full, incremental) as well as manage what gets backed up, when it gets backed up, and how often. File copying is a more manual process.

2. What's the difference between disk imaging and file-based backup?

Image-based backup will back up all of the drives in the computer by taking an exact image of them. This includes all data, applications, and the operating system. A file-and directory-based backup typically backs up the data only. When it comes to recovering a crashed computer system, image-based backups have the advantage since you get the whole restore in one step. File and directory backups have a slight advantage if you are only trying to recover a deleted file or directory.

3. What's the difference between online and offline backup?

Online backup will back up your data to the cloud (data center). Offline backup typically backs up your data to a different device at the same location. Needless to say, in the event of

a building-destroying disaster, it is better to have your data offsite.

    4. What's the difference between full backup, incremental backup, differential backup?

A full backup solution backs up all your data every time a backup is run. Incremental backup takes one full backup and then backs up all changes incrementally on each backup iteration. A differential backup takes a full backup, then on each iteration backs up all changes in regards to the original full backup. These different types of backup strategies are particularly important when doing a restore. In order of ease-of-restore it goes full, differential and then incremental.

    5. How can I ensure the safety of my company's sensitive data off-site?

Choose an accredited data center. The latest accreditation is SSAE 16. See *FAQ 7* for more detail on this.

    6. What are the companies using the business continuity service for?

Companies use this type of service to make sure they can have their computer infrastructure up and running in a relatively short amount of time. The ramifications of not doing so are severe and are covered in detail in this book.

    7. Isn't a backup tape with my data enough to protect my business from a disaster?

In most cases, no. Tapes are prone to failure due to the mechanical nature of this solution. They are also very sensitive to environmental conditions such as heat and humidity and are easy to lose and more likely to be stolen.

8. I am backing up my application data. Doesn't that mean that I am protected?

Not fully protected. In the event of a system or drive crash or, worse, some type of disaster, you would have to restore the operating system, all of the applications, and then finally the application data. This is a long, cumbersome process and often the media containing the applications cannot be located.

9. What are the benefits and advantages of online data backup?

The benefit of online backup is having a copy of your data in a geographically different location in the event of fire, flood. or any other disaster, which may damage or demolish your site.

10. What's the difference between business continuity, risk management, and emergency planning?

Risk management and emergency planning are both parts of business continuity.

11. What are the costs and benefits of migrating to a cloud service?

The costs as well as the benefits vary from situation to situation, but in most cases cloud

services, whether backup only or full cloud solutions, tend to be more fault tolerant as they are typically hosted in enterprise-level data centers.

12. Is business continuity plan worth the effort and the cost?

   In a word, Yes!

Myths

1. Firewalls and anti-virus software will fully protect my computer.

Firewalls and anti-virus software will help keep out malware and unwanted traffic but do not fully protect your system. You still need some type of backup solution in the event of a hardware or software malfunction.

2. Replicating your backups off-site requires expensive "WAN acceleration" technology.

Not true. Most online backup solutions run over standard Internet connections. And the speed of the Internet connections are getting faster by the day as well as less expensive.

3. People with local backups don't need cloud backups.

False. If a site burns down or floods, ruining all equipment, the backup data is also ruined. Having cloud (online) backups as part of your strategy is critical.

4. I have insurance that covers a business loss - it's called interruption insurance.

That may be true for a new building and new systems, but what about your data?

5. We've got backups, so we're ready for any disaster.

Backups are just one piece of a disaster recovery or business continuity solution. Without the rest, the recovery of your data would be not enough to keep your business running.

6. We can just back up some files and store them in the safe deposit box at our local bank.

This is better than no offsite back up but, again, not nearly a complete strategy to assure a quick return to business operations in the event of a disaster—whether it be natural or manmade.

7. Small to medium sized business don't need business continuity and disaster recovery solutions.

Small and medium sized businesses account for most businesses in this country. Regardless of the size of your business, if you can't afford to be down for more than a day (and I can tell you that most businesses can't) then business continuity and disaster recovery planning is essential.

8. Only financial services or healthcare organizations need business continuity solutions. My business doesn't fall under either category, therefore, I don't need a business continuity solution.

As we state above, there is much more to consider than the type of business. All businesses (in our opinion) need disaster recovery and business continuity plans in

place.

9. Cloud backups are too expensive and not secure.

The price of cloud-based backup is getting more affordable by the day and can now very closely compete with local-based solutions, especially if you give value to functionality and security. Additionally, most cloud backup solutions are exponentially more secure than anything that we can afford locally.

10. I can't have both security and convenience.

Sure you can.

11. My hard drive is under a 5-year warranty.

That's great but what about your data?

12. We have a small nonprofit organization. It won't matter if our office is closed for a few weeks.

What happens if you can't ever recover your client databases, donation records, and other protected data?

How to Find Out If You Are at Risk from a Potential Data Loss

Susan: What do you suggest for someone who thinks they have a sound system in place but wants to be sure they are protected?

Domenic: Many IT support companies offer a business continuity assessment at low cost. We typically offer them for free.

Depending on the size of the company, the report could be between 10 and 50 pages. It would describe exactly where the business is in terms of business continuity as well as other security-related factors. We do a penetration test on the network to make sure unwanted traffic cannot get through. So the business continuity assessment is the major component of the security assessment we provide.

Take advantage of this type of assessment. It can reveal gaps in your structure for only the investment of your time.

Susan: Okay, great then. Well, I want to say thank you, Domenic, because I think a lot of people just do not give this topic the love it deserves. We want to play with the data, but we don't want to think about what would happen if we lost that data.

Advances in technology have made the problem harder to manage, but at the same time, as you explained, have lowered the cost for an organization to make sure that, should the worst of the worst happen, they will come out of it okay.

Domenic: Absolutely correct. The cost is relative, I guess, but the flip side of the coin is hundreds of thousand times more expensive than just protecting yourself in the first place. I can add up these scary facts, and we already went through them, but I will do it again. Each company at 20 users is going to experience 1.7 unplanned outage events per year, so almost two a year. That's an average, so pretty much every company.

Each of those events is going to last almost seven hours. The Industry average from Aberdeen, which is a pretty good source, estimates $9,000/per hour of downtime and this is for the small company without adjustment for lost of revenue. When you look at loss of productivity, loss of data, loss of sales, loss of reputation and credibility, maybe loss of employee morale, the cost is very high. The reality is that it does not always happen to the other guy. It really does not. I know that to be true because I am taking care of the other guy every single day.

Susan: How can they get in touch with you if they have questions?

Domenic: They can check the website, www.backupfanatic.com. They can email me at dom@backupfanatic.com. They can check us out on Facebook or LinkedIn.

Here Is How to Ensure Your Business Is Protected from Disaster

You already know we live in a rapidly changing, technology-dependent world. Should the unthinkable happen, do you know how long it would take to get your company back online if there were a fire, flood, or other natural or man-made disaster at your main office?

That is where we come in. We help people just like you ensure your business is protected from all threats by delivering continuous protection, secure storage, data compliance, instant data recovery, and a multi-layered strategy regarding malware protection.

Here is a high-level breakdown of our methodology:

Step 1: We do a needs analysis, which includes but is not limited to a business continuity assessment, which includes a disaster recovery component to see how prepared you are with regard to your data backup and recovery.

Step 2: We help you uncover where you are vulnerable by doing a penetration test on your network to make sure you are safe and protected from hackers, and we also do a malware protection assessment.

Step 3: We take it from here and design a Business Continuation Assessment Report that will inform you how to protect your organization's IT resources when the next disaster strikes.

Most people think that because they back up every night their organization is safe. That is just not correct.

Now you can ensure your business is protected from all types of disasters; even the ones that have not yet been invented.

If you would like us to help, check us out at:

www.backupfanatic.com or simply send an email to: dom@backupfanatic.com and we will take it from there.

Protecting Your Personal Data... True, Hard Facts About Data Loss

- ✓ The average failure rate of disk and tape drives is 100% - ALL DRIVES WILL EVENTUALLY FAIL.

- ✓ Only 34% of companies test their tape backups, and of those who do, 77% have found failures.

- ✓ 60% of companies that lose their data will go out of business within 6 months of the disaster.

- ✓ Over ½ of critical corporate data resides on unprotected PC desktops and laptops.

- ✓ Key causes for data loss are:
    - o 78% Hardware or system malfunction
    - o 11% Human error
    - o 7% Software corruption or program malfunction
    - o 2% Computer viruses
    - o 1% Natural disasters
    - o 1% Other

- ✓ Only 25% of users frequently back up their

files, yet 85% of those same users say they are very concerned about losing important digital data.

- ✓ More than 22% said backing up their PCs was on their to-do list, but they seldom do it.

- ✓ 30% of companies report that they still do not have a disaster recovery program in place, and two out of three feel their data backup and disaster recovery plans have significant vulnerabilities.

- ✓ 1 in 25 notebooks are stolen, broken or destroyed each year.

- ✓ Today's hard drives store 500 times the data stored on the drives of a decade ago. This increased capacity amplifies the impact of data loss, making mechanical precision more critical.

- ✓ You have a 30% chance of having a corrupted file within a one-year time frame.

*Source: VaultLogix

I don't know about you but these facts certainly got my attention. Like it or not, we store a ton of data on our home PC's. From pictures of the grandkids and financial information to the spreadsheet from work, we had better learn to protect that data.

Additionally, most of us do banking from our home PC, not to mention all those purchases from Amazon where we are sharing our credit and debit card information.

Having said all of that, let's talk about four ways that you can have a safer home computing experience and keep that important data backed up too.

1. Backup, Backup, Backup – There are hundreds of inexpensive (and in some cases free) software programs out there that are built specifically to back up your home data. To start, let's list a few that are built right into the operating system. With Microsoft comes One Drive. Simply copy the files that you want to back up to the "One Drive" and you're done. Of course, if you don't copy the files they will not get backed up. For Apple devices there is iCloud. Same type of thing. Just copy the files over. Both of these solutions are Cloud-based (offsite) backups, so if your device is stolen or dies or in a fire or flood, a copy of your key files will be offsite in the Microsoft and Apple Clouds, respectively. A few commercial inexpensive products that work with both Macs and Windows-based PC's are Carbonite and Mozy. The major advantage to these programs is that you can automatically set the folders that you want backed up once, and both products will keep all files in these folders backed up without any user actions necessary. This is a critical feature, as we tend to forget and the less human intervention necessary, the better. Another strategy for backing up your critical files is to use one of the file-sync software products such as Dropbox, BOX or Google Drive. These are particularly useful

if you use more than one device and want to keep your key files synched across all of your devices. This allows you to get a backup of these files as they simultaneously live on more than one device. Different products will fit different people's needs but it is critical that you choose one of them or something similar. Lastly and MOST IMPORTANTLY, do test restores of various files at regular intervals. I would say weekly would be a good strategy for most of us. Let's remember. Backups are meaningless if we can't recover the data!

2. Anti-Malware Software – If you have ever been affected by a virus, then you will know what a pain it can be to clean it. The symptoms can range anywhere from harmless popups and/or slow system performance to having all of your data wiped or, arguably worse, your credit card and bank information stolen. We can go a long way in protecting ourselves by having a good antimalware software installed on our systems and making sure we update the virus signatures (it is best to set the software to automatically download and install these updates as the human error factor can also play here, as well as with backup). There are numerous products out there. We tend to use Kaspersky or ESET most of the time and, in our opinion, these do the best job at protecting systems from today's various forms of malware. They are relatively inexpensive and certainly worth what you spend on them. If, however, you

can't afford it, there are plenty of decent free programs out there, including Microsoft's Security Essentials. Regardless of what software you decide on, it is critical to use some common sense when computing. For example, I use an email SPAM filter that keeps the junk (and some malware) out of my inbox, I never click on or open any attachment in an email that I am not expecting, I seldom open emails if I do not recognize the sender, and I NEVER click links inside of an email unless I am 100% sure of them and had been expecting them. Finally, I always keep my malware software updated and do regular schedule scans on my computers.

3. Firewalls (Hardware and Software) – To keep this really simple, a firewall is something that keeps out unwanted traffic. Most businesses use hardware-based firewalls as well as software-based firewalls on the PC's. Most home users use strictly software-based firewalls. Typically, they come as part of your antimalware suite and block unknown and unwanted traffic as well as protect against various phishing attacks meant to steal our personal information. In the event that your antimalware software does not include a firewall, Microsoft operating systems come with a firewall built in called Windows Firewall. I strongly encourage you to keep this enabled if you aren't protected in other ways.

4. Patching – It is arguably as important or

more important to keep your operating systems and all applications updated with latest patches. Both Microsoft and Apple, as well as most software products, make it easy to do so by offering the options to automate the process. I strongly urge you to do so.

It can be a big, scary computing world out there, but we can do much to protect ourselves by using a little common sense and a little discipline in our computing habits.

Epilogue

March 22, 2015

It's Sunday morning at 10AM.

It's been about five weeks since I wrote the prologue to this book.

In those five weeks a lot has happened.

Boston had its snowiest season ever with 108 inches of snow, most of which fell in February. Many people have not been able to get to work and there has been an enormous cost to productivity overall.

Companies who were able to offer offsite access and who could backup and incorporate mobile file data into their normal operations did very, very well.

Companies that had an incomplete business continuity plan saw those plans tested.

Companies who hoped for the best rather than plan for the worst, learned the hard way.

It is your job to make certain your business can operate with compromised infrastructure or limited employee access.

Make sure you backup your families photos first though. And as you now know, make sure you test restore them. Take care of what you value!

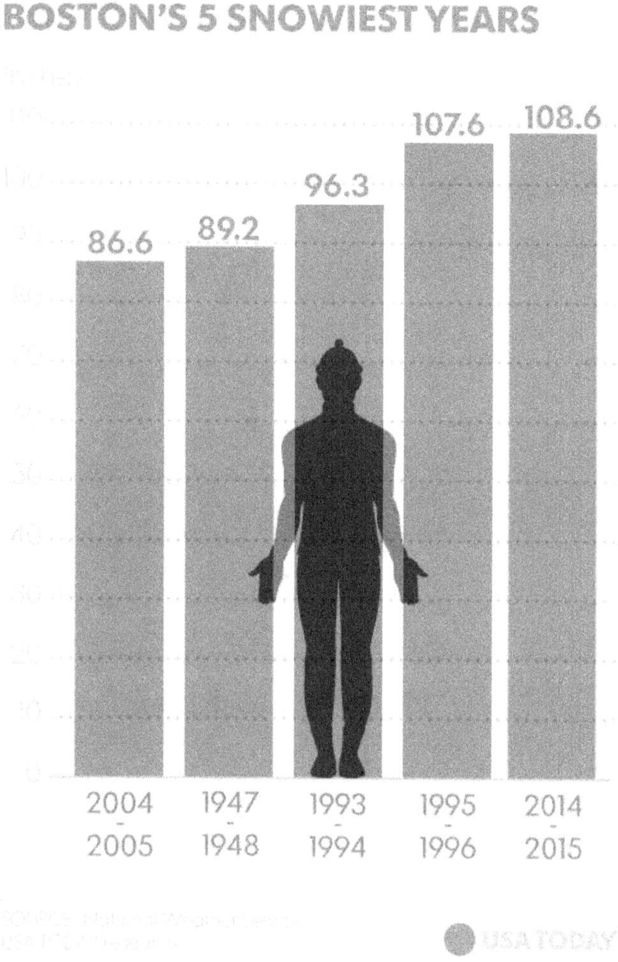

BOSTON'S 5 SNOWIEST YEARS

	86.6	89.2	96.3	107.6	108.6
	2004–2005	1947–1948	1993–1994	1995–1996	2014–2015

Some things to think about:

- IHS Global Insight, an economic analysis firm, estimates Massachusetts alone suffered roughly $1 billion in lost wages and profits, as storm after storm pummeled the region, delivering more than 8 feet of snow in roughly a month.

- The snowstorms caused sales to fall an average of 24 percent for many industries surveyed by Massachusetts business groups. Payroll fell approximately seven percent for small business members.

- "We still have congested streets and longer commutes and that's meaning lost productivity," said Timothy Murray, president of the Worcester Regional Chamber of Commerce. "The system has really been no match for Mother Nature."

- Economists expect the ripple effects of New England's storms will be felt nationally, but it's too early to say to what extent.

- Not to mention the hundreds if not thousands of local business shutdowns this winter due to weather related issues.

- The MBTA finally re-opened and is running on time. Well, as on time as they ever run.

So, to finish where we started. It does not take a hurricane, fire, flood or any of the other natural or manmade disasters to bring down our businesses. This winter has proved this point once again. Lack of access is just as devastating.

About the Author

With 25+ years of experience in the information technology field, Mr. DiSario is the President of Business Solutions Unplugged, Inc. He has worked his way up through the industry starting out in the early 1980's as a PC Tech. He became a Certified NetWare Engineer (CNE) and has designed and implemented PC Networks and vertical solutions since 1988. While an independent contractor for various network service companies, Mr. DiSario went on to become one of the first Novell Master CNE's. In the late eighties he began accruing his own client base, many of whom remain clients today.

As Microsoft entered the networking market, Mr. DiSario enhanced his skills to mirror the changing technology and became a Microsoft Certified Systems Engineer (MCSE), as well as a Compaq Accredited Systems Engineer(ASE), a Citrix Certified Engineer and a Microsoft Certified Trainer (MCT)

Mr. DiSario is recognized as an industry leader in local and wide area networking as well as remote access solutions and satellite office connectivity for both large and small companies. He has lectured on networking at Boston University, served as adjunct faculty at Clark University, has been published in LAN Times and his company has been featured on WCVB TV's Chronicle.

Recently Mr. DiSario authored the book "Technology as a 2nd Language" which has been cited on all of the major broadcasting networks and subsequently founded TA2L.COM whose target audience is seasoned business executives struggling to adapt to today's newer, technology-based methods of communicating. TA2L's books and coaching services offer practical, experience based guidance to help these professionals connect with clients, prospects and colleagues using the platforms and devices that their audiences prefer.

Most recently Mr. DiSario authored and published this book Backup Fanatic under the "Technology as a 2nd Language" series

Look for his next release " Meditations for Geeks" due out at the end of 2015.

Postscript

I can't resist an "I told you so". We were just about to submit this book to the publisher and coincidentally ran across this article in the Boston Globe.

Published in Boston Globe, Tuesday April 7, 2015

www.ingramcontent.com/pod-product-compliance
Lightning Source LLC
Chambersburg PA
CBHW051723170526
45167CB00002B/776